GARDENING S

by Dr Margaret Vickery

Edited by David Dunbar

This book is dedicated to the memory of the late Mr Robert Kiln, who was in his lifetime a strong supporter of Butterfly Conservation. It is published through the generosity of his family and friends.

BUTTERFLY
CONSERVATION

PUBLISHED BY THE BRITISH BUTTERFLY CONSERVATION SOCIETY LTD

PO BOX 222, DEDHAM, NR COLCHESTER, ESSEX CO7 6EY
01206 322342

ISBN NO: 0 9522602 6 3

CONTENTS

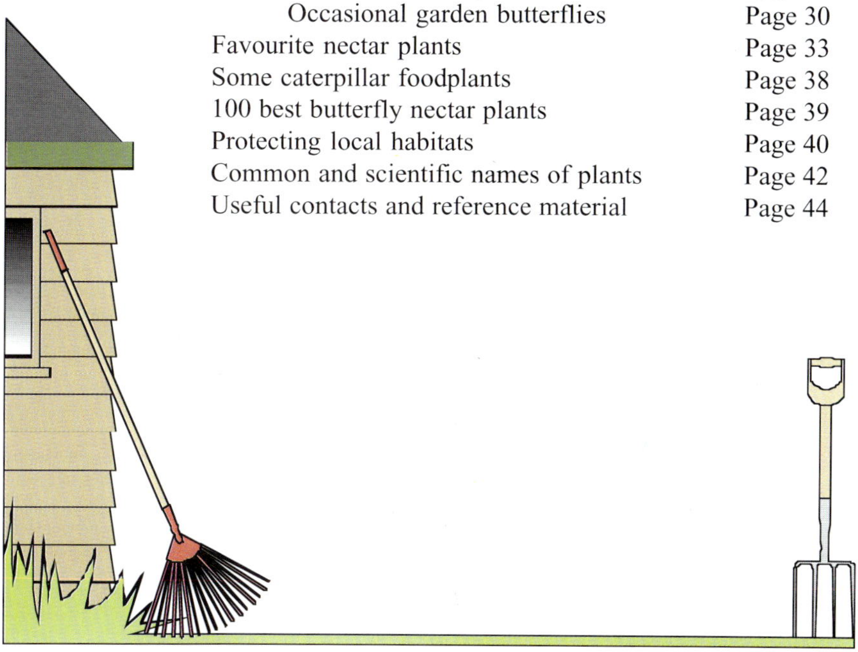

GARDENING FOR BUTTERFLIES

PREFACE

Butterfly Conservation's first *Gardening for Butterflies* booklet, written by Madge Payne ten years ago, has been one of our most popular publications, inspiring many gardeners and even non-gardeners to plant for butterflies.

Since publication of the first edition, Butterfly Conservation has been running a garden butterfly survey which started in 1990. Over the first five years the analysis of more than 2500 recording forms gave us much new knowledge about the behaviour and needs of butterflies visiting gardens, including the effects of shade, shelter, aspect and surroundings and the importance of nectar plants. These results have been incorporated into this new edition.

ACKNOWLEDGEMENTS

I would first like to thank Madge Payne for writing such an excellent first edition and so making my task much easier than it would have been if I'd had to start from scratch.

My grateful thanks go to Jon Holmes for revising the garden plans and to the staff of the Conservation Office for making many useful comments and changes to the original manuscript.

I would also like to thank David Dunbar for his editing work and most of the excellent photographs throughout this book, Maggie Thurgood for the design and layout, and Martyn Davies and the Information & Education Committee for publishing this booklet.

Finally, on behalf of Butterfly Conservation I must pay tribute to all the garden butterfly survey recorders whose painstaking efforts over the years have enabled this booklet to be written.

Margaret Vickery
January 1998

WHY GARDEN FOR BUTTERFLIES?

Gardens are an ideal place to watch butterflies. Hours of enjoyment can be had observing these beautiful creatures flitting from flower to flower. A visit from a new species is always a delight and familiar visitors are welcomed back each year.

To garden for butterflies is neither back-breaking nor expensive and the results are well worth the effort involved. Butterflies are the flowers of the sky adding a third dimension of delight as they dance over the flowers of the earth.

Natural habitat for wild creatures has disappeared at an alarming rate during the second half of the twentieth century. Industrial and housing developments, roads and intensive farming have all taken their toll, devouring the woods and fields where butterflies once flew in peace and tranquillity.

Gardens are not, and never can be, substitutes for the countryside but they can be an important element in the survival of butterflies and other wildlife on our overcrowded islands.

Although it may seem that there are many nature reserves across the British Isles, they are widely scattered and separated from one another by roads, towns, housing estates and cultivated fields. Most butterflies are unable to fly far without stopping to rest and feed on nectar to provide energy for the next stage of the journey. Gardens can act as important stepping stones between nature reserves and other natural habitat by offering abundant supplies of nectar.

Gardens are even more important during times of drought, such as we have experienced in recent years. Our national garden butterfly survey recorded far more butterflies in well watered gardens when the drought had killed most of the wild nectar flowers in the countryside.

Buddleia, the Butterfly Bush, is guaranteed to attract

NATIONAL GARDEN BUTTERFLIES SURVEY

This survey, co-ordinated by Butterfly Conservation, has been running since 1990.

Analysis of the data has helped to establish the characteristics of the garden most likely to attract butterflies, for example:-

- Gardens should be open to the sun and, if possible, surround the house.
- It is an advantage to be situated in the countryside and near at least three different types of wild habitat eg woodland, flower-rich grassland, disused railway line etc.
- Larger gardens generally attract more species.
- Most important of all, the garden should contain over 30 different kinds of nectar plant.

Few gardens have all these characteristics, but all can contain a good selection of nectar plants, which is the most important factor in attracting butterflies.

Gardens in the north may not attract as many butterfly species, as fewer species extend their range so far and the weather is likely to be less butterfly-friendly! Although gardens in the countryside were found overall to be better at attracting butterflies than those in towns or the suburbs, this was not always true when individual gardens were compared. Provided butterflies are breeding within flying distance, a good suburban or town garden can attract a surprising number of species.

The main purpose of the survey now is to monitor the health and well-being of the commoner butterflies and to discover more about their behaviour, as there is still much to learn even for these common species.
(To take part in the survey contact Butterfly Conservation.)

A natural mixture of wild flowers and grasses

ORGANIC GARDENING

One of the reasons why butterflies disappeared from gardens in the 1950-70s was the indiscriminate use of insecticides and other pesticides.

Gardeners are now coming to realise the harm such products can cause to all living creatures.

By using only natural products and allowing nature to create a balance between pests and their predators a garden full of wildlife interest can be achieved, albeit one in which the occasional slug or snail-chewed leaf will be encountered.

It is rare in an organically managed garden for pests to completely destroy plants, and it is worth tolerating some damage in exchange for the many enthralling birds, insects and other creatures which will make such a garden their abode.

Most garden centres now stock organic fertilisers made from natural sources, such as chicken manure pellets, which I find very successful, even if they do have a strong smell!

Good garden centres also stock peat-free products, which butterfly lovers will want to use, as the extraction of peat destroys the habitat of several butterfly species, such as the Large Heath, as well as a wealth of other specialised wildlife.

You can make your own compost from grass cuttings and weeds (but not perennial weeds like dandelion, as the heat of the compost heap may not kill them) and from vegetable peelings etc.

Flower-rich grassland attracts many species

Creating a compost heap is simple - I just let mine rot down in a corner of the garden, transferring it to a plastic dustbin for its final conversion to humus. This is used in pots and tubs and as a mulch around the garden.

Further advice on making compost at home can be obtained from Henry Doubleday Research Association *(address on page 44).*

MAKING A BUTTERFLY GARDEN

Butterflies are said to be cold-blooded and need a certain amount of warmth before they become active and can fly. As soon as they are mobile they will search for the warmest, sheltered spot to bask in the sun's rays and then find a nectar source. If they can combine the two then so much the better.

Making a garden attractive to butterflies is not difficult, nor does it mean you and your neighbours have to put up with lots of weeds and general untidiness.

The best butterfly gardens mimic the old cottage gardens, which were full of annual and perennial plants massed together, producing a rich source of nectar for butterflies and other insects.

A large enough garden could include a wild area, and this is an obvious advantage. However, growing some of the attractive wild plants, such as scabious, knapweed, marjoram, common fleabane, and bird's-foot trefoil, amongst cultivated varieties is almost as successful in attracting butterflies, provided they are breeding not too far away.

Some species will breed in gardens if the correct caterpillar foodplants are provided in the right habitat, such as an area of wildflower grassland. Female Orange Tip butterflies will lay eggs on cuckoo flower (lady's smock), dame's violet (sweet rocket) or honesty. Others are mentioned further on.

Having chosen which type of garden you wish to have, it is important to identify the warmest and sunniest places in spring and autumn. This is where plants that will flower at those times should be grown if they are to benefit the butterflies that hibernate over winter.

Avoid large expanses of spring flowers at the expense of summer and autumn ones because spring-flying butterflies are usually less numerous than those appearing later in the summer.

During the mid-summer months, the sun extends into more parts of the garden and

Ice plant flower heads covered with different butterfly visitors

so summer plants can be grown in these sun-exposed beds.

Summer flowering plants may often go where the spring flowers have finished and been cleared away. Wallflowers and forget-me-nots can be completely changed at the beginning of June to make way for a suitable display of bedding plants.

The flowering period of summer plants can often be extended by the regular removal of dead blooms until the plants are finally killed by Autumn frosts. The flowering period of hardy annuals can also be prolonged by sowing a few seeds at fortnightly intervals throughout April and May.

Shelter and Warmth

A cold, windswept, overshadowed, north-facing garden does not attract butterflies, especially if it is planted with unsuitable things such as rhododendrons, roses, lilies and gladioli. One is likely to see only the occasional butterfly en route to a warmer, sunnier place where there are good nectar flowers to be found.

Exposed gardens can be improved by the cultivation of shrubs and trees on the northern boundaries.

A hedge is superior to a wall for reducing the damaging effects of a strong wind, the shelter band being approximately four times the height of the hedge. Privet, laurel, hawthorns and holly, if allowed to grow to a flowering height, will create good windbreaks and nectar too.

A mixed garden hedge provides shelter- nasturtium at the base is a good caterpillar foodplant

Fences and walls will obviously give good shelter as well but conifer hedges are not recommended as they do not provide butterfly nectar. It has been suggested that the resinous smell exuded by conifers in summer may deter some butterflies.

Providing winter homes

Several garden visitors spend the winter in hibernation, including Small Tortoiseshell, Peacock, Comma and

Avoiding the use of pesticides allows a natural balance

Brimstone, so the provision of places to hide in, such as hedges, or ivy or other evergreen climbers growing up a fence or wall will mean early spring butterflies in the garden.

Avoid pesticides

Having provided for your butterfly visitors, don't accidentally kill them by using pesticides in the garden!

Any pesticide can be dangerous, whatever it says on the label.

It is far better to grit your teeth during the emergence of greenfly in the spring and wait for the arrival of ladybirds, hover flies and all the other insects that feed on these pests.

If left alone, nature will always eventually achieve a balance and you will have much more wildlife to watch in the garden.

You can help to keep pests away from your vegetables by, for example, planting nasturtiums amongst cabbages and marigolds with beans. In fact the old cottage gardeners often mixed up flowers and vegetables to the benefit of both.

Caring for your plants

To keep your garden attractive to butterflies over the years, remove any plants that are not thriving and fill in the gaps.

Some perennials may need dividing every few years. Most annuals will seed themselves, but will need 'topping up' from time to time. A light dressing of organic fertiliser, such as farmyard or stable manure, chicken manure pellets, or home-made compost will keep the plants healthy, but not too much or flowers will be sacrificed for leaves.

Above all, water, water, water during a drought, using rain water collected in a water butt and all the waste water from the kitchen if a hose pipe ban has been imposed. Plants suffering from drought either do not produce nectar or make it too thick for butterflies to drink through the hollow tubes in their tongues.

THE SMALL GARDEN

Making a small garden attractive to butterflies is not difficult or expensive and the result can be a charming oasis of scent and colour.

Ideally, the garden should be bounded by a high fence, wall or hedge on the northern and eastern sides to provide shelter from cold winds and to form the basis of the edge-type habitat which is so attractive to butterflies.

A plot open to the south is best but even a north facing garden can be successful, although there will be an area in front of the house that will be in shadow throughout most of the day. It would be pointless to grow nectar plants in this area, but it makes a pleasant, cool place to sit and watch butterflies in a heatwave!

Fences and walls can be covered in climbing plants such as clematis, honeysuckle and everlasting pea. Ivy is a very useful plant to grow as it is evergreen and provides hiding places for butterflies to rest overnight and to hibernate in the winter. If it is allowed to flower, ivy will attract the females of the Holly Blue into your garden, where, hopefully, they will lay eggs on the flower buds.

Ivy flowers are good sources of nectar in late autumn and attract other butterflies, especially Red Admirals, as well as many moths. You can encourage ivy to produce flowering stems by pulling the top shoots away from their support, so that they hang free.

In the spring the Holly Blue lays eggs on the flower buds of holly. There are slow growing varieties of holly available from garden centres, ideal for small gardens, but make sure you buy a female bush.

PLANTING PLANS FOR SMALL GARDENS

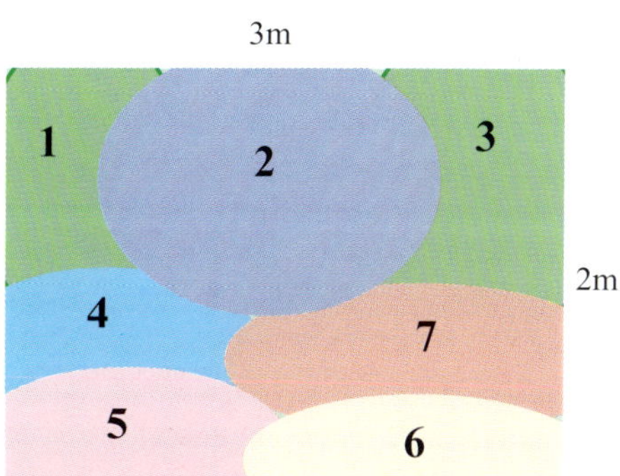

1 Honesty
2 Buddleia nanhoensis blue underplanted with primroses
3 Field scabious
4 Marjoram
5 Candytuft
6 Drumstick primulas
7 Statice (summer) and Wallflowers (spring)

The best type of hedge to have is one made up of several wild flowering shrubs, but this is generally not practicable in a small garden. If a single species hedge is planted, make it privet and cut as little as possible during the growing season so that flowers are produced. Privet flowers are rich in nectar and attract many butterflies, including Comma and Red Admiral and even, possibly, Purple Hairstreak and White-letter Hairstreak.

To create the edge-type habitat found along woodland rides or at the boundary of hedge and meadow you will need to plant as many nectar producing plants as possible in front of your fence, wall or hedge (although not too close to hedge roots, as these will take both water and nutrients from the soil).

Our research has shown that the more different types of plant that are grown the more chance there is of encouraging a large number of butterfly species to visit your garden. Choose plants that together will give a flowering time extending from early spring to late autumn. In a small garden this will mean not growing more that one or two of each type. This is quite satisfactory for perennials which are natural spreaders and self-seeders, such as marjoram.

Annual bedding plants such as French marigolds and candytuft need to be planted in larger groups and if there is not room in the garden, grow these plants in tubs placed amongst the perennials or at the edge of a lawn, path or patio.

Placing tubs in the centre of open spaces, such as a mown lawn or patio is not so successful, possibly because butterflies are more conspicuous to predators when exposed in this way. They need a dense mass of plants to

PLANTING PLANS FOR SMALL GARDENS

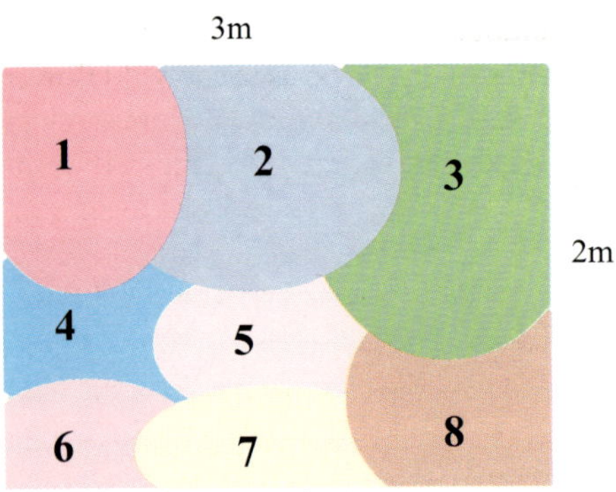

1 Phlox paniculata (pink)
2 Field scabious interplanted with Knapweed
3 Sweet rocket
4 Forget-me-not
5 Lavendar Hidcote
6 Annual scabious
7 French marigolds (summer) and Primulas (spring)
8 Candytuft

A newly planted buddleia avenue

provide camouflage and instant cover. Plant as close together as possible, so that the amount of bare earth visible is minimal - remember, though that most perennials spread.

Large expanses of bare earth have the same deterrent effect on butterflies as mown lawns. When planting in front of a fence or wall, place the tallest plants at the back and the lowest, such as thyme and bird's-foot trefoil, at the junction of border and lawn or path. If you have a choice, make your butterfly border so that it faces south or west.

Every butterfly garden, be it large or small, must have at least one buddleia bush. This should be given the sunniest spot and treated with a lot of loving care. Your reward will be a continuous stream of butterflies during the flowering season, whenever the sun is shining. To keep the nectar flowing each bush needs a bucket of water a day during a drought and to extend the flowering season the dead spikes should be removed every two or three days. A buddleia bush left to its own devices will not produce good quality flowers after the first year or two. It must be vigorously pruned every year at the end of February or beginning of March. And I do mean vigorously!

Whilst making sure that enough leaves are left to feed the new growth, most of the larger bushes can be cut down to half their summer height or even less. Old, dead wood should also be removed. Many bushes produce strong, new shoots from ground level to replace old, dead tissue and thus the life of a bush can be 20 or more years. To prevent winter wind and snow damage, the bush can be given a light pruning in the autumn, after flowering.

Although it is not possible to have a wild flower meadow in a small garden, some wild flowers can be included in the perennial border or a small area can be used as a wild flower bed. Plants that are both attractive to look at and attractive to butterflies include knapweed, scabious, marjoram, lady's smock (cuckoo flower), primrose and bird's-foot trefoil. The latter will attract Common Blue butterflies, if there are any breeding near your garden, as it is both a good nectar plant and the caterpillar foodplant.

LARGE GARDENS

All that has been said about small and town gardens also applies to large gardens, but advantage can be taken of the opportunity to create areas of more natural habitat.

A wild area can be created by sowing a wild flower/grass seed mixture on bare ground, or individual wild flower plants can be set amongst existing grass.

In the latter case dig a patch free of grass which is a few inches bigger than the plant plug to help the plant become established and make sure that tall grasses are not shutting out the light.

You will need to establish a cutting regime according to the species that come to breed within this wild area. If unsure when to cut, opt for late September/early October and make sure that the cuttings are raked off the area, but do not burn them. If the cuttings are left in a corner, any butterfly eggs, hibernating caterpillar or chrysalis will have a chance of surviving

Large gardens provide an opportunity to create a wild area

It is also possible to have an 'ideal' nettle patch in a large garden. This is a large patch of nettles which are growing in full sun in a sheltered position and which are well fed with nitrogenous fertiliser, preferably natural manure, and kept watered during a drought.

Such a nettle patch will provide a breeding area for Small Tortoisehells, Peacocks, Red Admirals and Commas. Each of these species has different needs: for Small Tortoiseshells new growth is essential and so part of the nettle patch should be cut as soon as the first adults of the new brood appear in late June/ early July. Peacocks produce only one brood which do not emerge until late July or August. These butterflies hibernate overwinter and lay their eggs on spring nettles.

In our national garden butterfly survey, large gardens generally attracted more species of butterfly than small ones, but this was not invariably so.

Large gardens can have a number of disadvantages, the worst being extensive areas of mown grass, or of bare earth or paths, and beds of modern, nectarless varieties of plants, such as roses or other shrubs.

It is possible to mitigate such deterrents by planting a wide nectar corridor from one end of the garden to the other, preferably south facing in front of a hedge, wall or fence giving shelter from north and east winds.

Use a mixture of plants listed on page 39 and if the edges of such borders are planted with low growing plants such as birds-foot trefoil and thyme which are allowed to spill over onto the adjacent lawn or path, they may attract the pretty Common Blue butterfly.

In chalk/limestone areas where the Chalkhill Blue occurs try growing horseshoe vetch too, and rockrose for Brown Argus.

An advantage of a large garden is the opportunity to create a natural hedge made up of indigenous trees and shrubs: oak for Purple Hairstreak; elm for White-letter Hairstreak (coppice this tree when the trunk becomes about 6 inches in diameter to prevent Dutch Elm disease getting a hold), and holly and ivy for Holly Blue.

If planting a hedge from scratch it would be worth while getting advice from your local wildlife trust on the species to plant. Old gardens often have an orchard and this can be made into valuable butterfly habitat. Sunny paths and open areas are essential, as is a good supply of nectar plants throughout the year. In autumn rotting windfalls will attract butterflies such as Comma and Red Admiral in their dozens!

PLANTING PLANS FOR MEDIUM-SIZED GARDENS

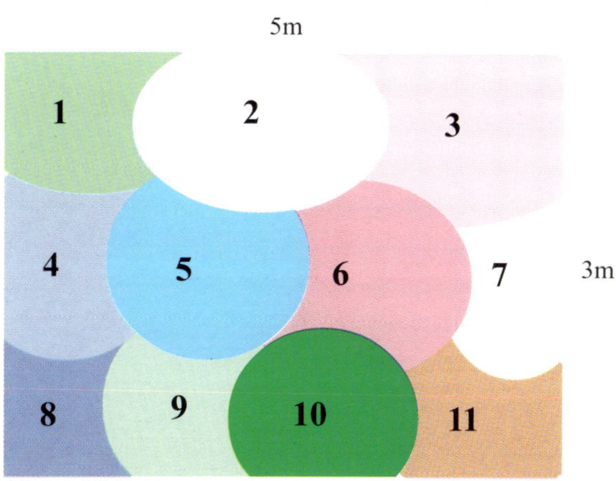

1 Teasel
2 Buddleia davidii White Profusion
3 Michaelmas daisy (pink)
4 Lavender Hidcote
5 Honesty
6 Phlox paniculata (pink)
7 Sweet rocket (white)
8 Drumstick primulas (violet)
9 Candytuft
10 Static interplanted with Verbena venosa
11 Heather

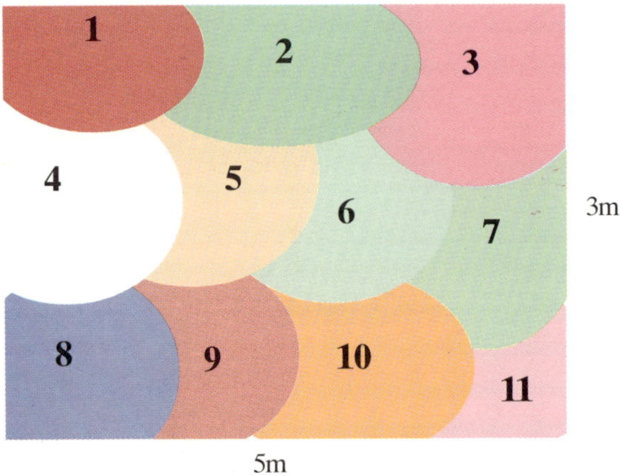

1 Buddleia nanhoensis Royal Red
2 Cornus alba variegata
3 Buddleia nanhoensis (purple) (underplant 1-3 with primroses)
4 Sweet rocket
5 Tansy
6 Field scabious
7 Marjoram
8 Aubretia (violet)
9 Ice plant
10 French marigolds (summer) Wallflowers (spring)
11 Lavender

A rock garden in the spring offering a colourful choice of nectar flowers

5m

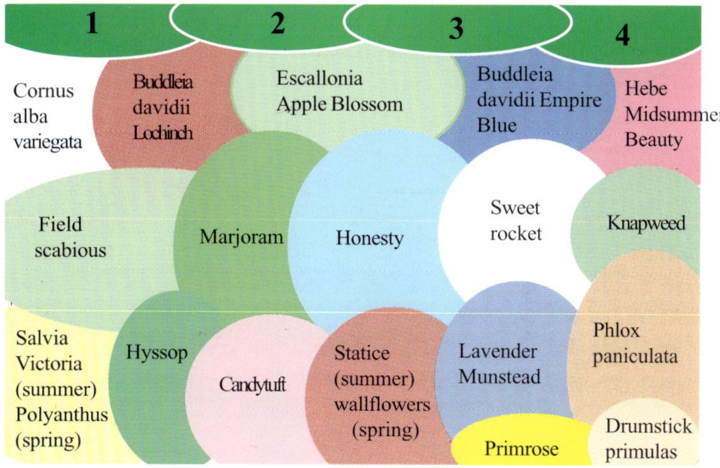

10m

The hedge along the back of the above border consists of:
1 Privet with honeysuckle 2 Buckthorn with everlasting pea 3 Hawthorn 4 Holly

10m

5m

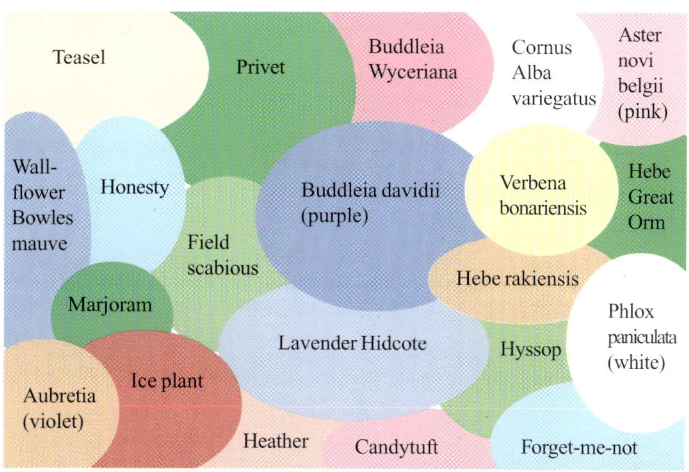

TOWN GARDENS

Even gardens in the heart of a town will have the occassional butterfly visitor, if full of nectar plants.

Small Tortoiseshells, Large and Small Whites and Brimstones commonly occur in town centres, while the migrant Painted Ladies and Red Admirals have been seen in the the most unlikely places. It is not unknown for very rare migrants such as the Clouded Yellow and Camberwell Beauty to be seen in towns!

Town gardens are usually small; maybe only a patio or window box is available. In the latter case, keep the box filled with nectar plants from spring to autumn, refilling several times during the butterfly season. Crocus, primrose and grape hyacinth in the early spring; pansies or violas for late spring; candytuft and Tagetes ('Naughty Marietta'), lobelia or alyssum for the summer and ice plant for autumn are possibilites, but do experiment. I have grown ice plant in a basket suspended on a fence facing south which attracted many Small Tortoiseshells and Red Admirals in October.

A patio or roof garden can be the equivalent of a five star restaurant for butterflies passing through towns.

Fill an area with tubs massed close together, rather than spread out with lots of bare stone between them, and crammed with nectar plants.

Again, it is worth experimenting with different combinations for a few years until you find the plants that work for your situation. I have found that tubs

PLANTING PLANS FOR CONTAINERS

Based on 60cm half barrel

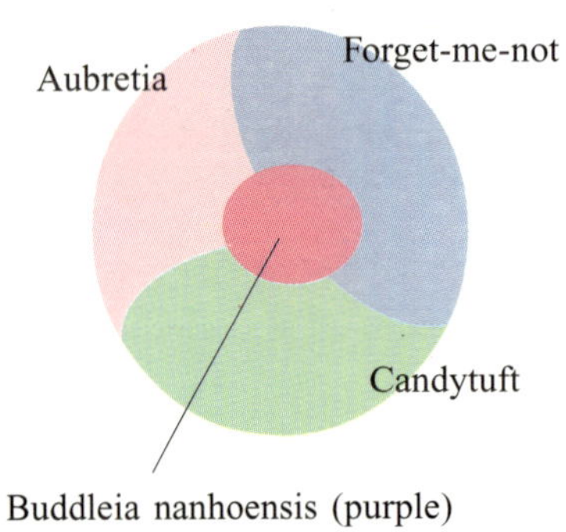

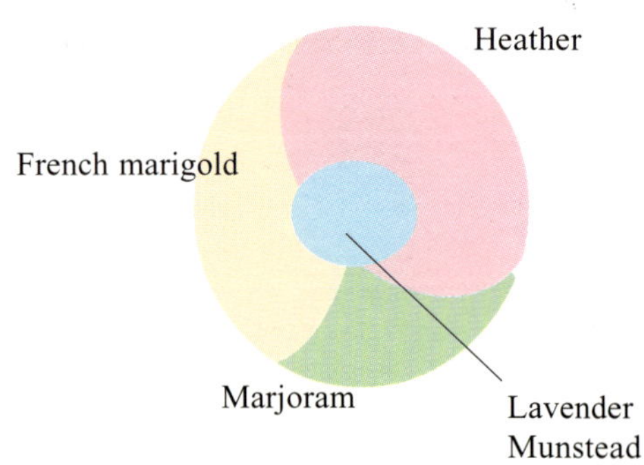

A sunny mixed flower border in August

planted with only one type of plant, eg the annuals candytuft or French marigold, or perennials such as origanum or Bowles mauve wallflower work better than those containing mixed plants.

Buddleias, especially the slender, smaller-leaved varieties can be grown in large tubs (prune very heavily every year) on a sunny patio. Remember that plants grown under these conditions need daily watering and regular feeding to produce nectar, and it goes without saying that the patio must be sheltered and in the sun for the greater part of the day. Be ruthless, too, and throw out any plants that are not thriving or are past their best and replant the tub. A butterfly patio garden can be just as expensive and keep you just as busy, as any other.

Other plants suitable for growing in containers:
African marigolds, Dahlia (Coltness hybrids), nasturtium, scabious (annual), drumstick primulas, primulas, wallflowers, thyme, Birds-foot trefoil, hebe, Phlox paniculata, Ice plant, Red valerian, stinging nettles

PLANTING PLANS FOR CONTAINERS

Based on 60cm half barrel

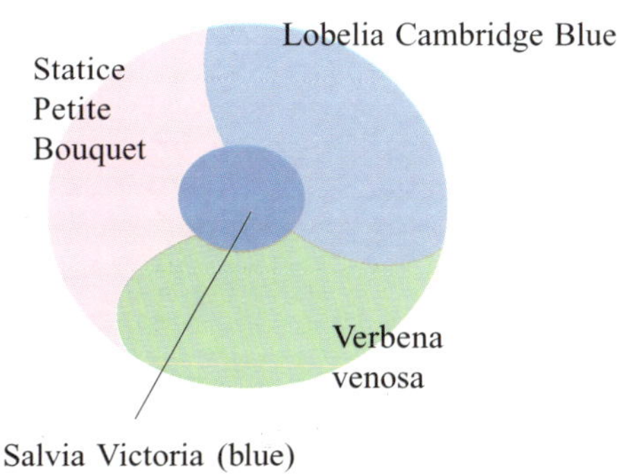

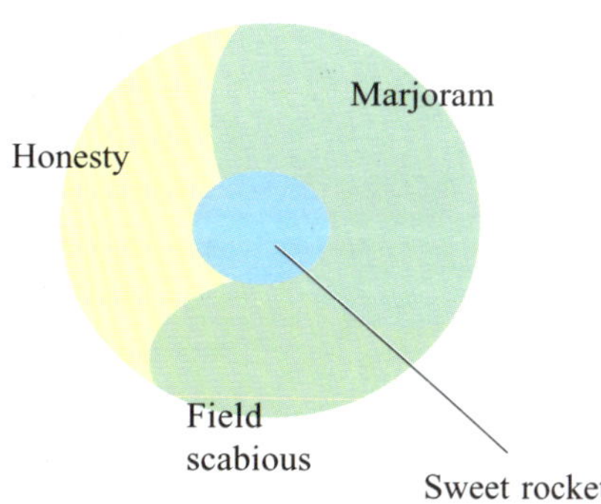

In Brief

- Plant as many different nectar plants as possible in sunny areas.
- Have at least one buddleia bush which is kept pruned.
- Mass plants with as little bare earth as possible.
- Keep plants well watered during a drought and remove dead flowers.
- Grow some caterpillar foodplants
- Avoid extensive pathed areas or mown lawns.
- If possible, provide shelter from cold north and east winds.

A midsummer flower bed designed for butterflies

GARDEN BUTTERFLIES

Our garden butterfly survey has found that a good butterfly garden, depending on its geographic location, can expect to have visits from up to 18 species of butterfly in most years, with a possibility of 22 for gardens in the southern half of Britain.

In a good year, the occasional large garden in the south which contains a wild flower meadow may manage as many as 28 - 30, but this is extremely rare.

In this chapter I shall describe the 22 species more generally seen.

One point established by our survey was that there are three distinct classes of garden visitor: those butterflies that are seen in almost all gardens (most widespread); those seen in a large number of gardens but by no means all (less widespread); and those seen every year but only in a few gardens (occasional).

MOST WIDESPREAD GARDEN BUTTERFLIES	Large White	*(Pieris brassicae)*
	Small White	*(Pieris rapae)*
	Red Admiral	*(Vanessa atalanta)*
	Small Tortoiseshell	*(Aglais urticae)*
	Peacock	*(Inachis io)*
LESS WIDESPREAD GARDEN BUTTERFLIES	Brimstone	*(Gonepteryx rhamni)*
	Green-veined White	*(Pieris napi)*
	Orange Tip	*(Anthocharis cardamines)*
	Common Blue	*(Polyommatus icarus)*
	Holly Blue	*(Celastrina argiolus)*
	Painted Lady	*(Cynthia cardui)*
	Comma	*(Polygonia c-album)*
	Speckled Wood	*(Pararge aegeria)*
	Gatekeeper	*(Pyronia tithonus)*
	Meadow Brown	*(Maniola jurtina)*
OCCASIONAL GARDEN BUTTERFLIES	Small Skipper	*(Thymelicus sylvestris)*
	Large Skipper	*(Ochlodes venata)*
	Small Copper	*(Lycaena phlaeas)*
	Wall Brown	*(Lasiommata megera)*
	Marbled White	*(Melanargia galathea)*
	Small Heath	*(Coenonympha pamphilus)*
	Ringlet	*(Aphantopus hyperantus)*

MOST WIDESPREAD GARDEN BUTTERFLIES

Five species are seen at some time of the year in most gardens: Large White, Small White, Red Admiral, Small Tortoiseshell and Peacock.

The **Large White** is to some extent a migrant from Europe but it breeds strongly in Britain, as anyone who grows cabbages will testify! Both the Large and Small White are also known as cabbage whites, as they both breed on members of the cabbage family.

The **Small White** is usually the first to be seen, generally flying in April but an early spring can produce individuals in March. There are few to be seen in early July and then the second brood appears at the end of July or the beginning of August. This butterfly occurs throughout Britain but is rare in the Scottish Islands.

Large White

Favourite plants
Lavender, Runner bean, Lobelia, Aubretia, Honesty, Michaelmas daisy, Field scabious, Marjoram, Catmint, Phlox, Purple loosestrife, Wallflower, Verbena, Nasturtium

Small White

Favourite plants
Lavender, Aubretia, Marjoram, Red valerian, Honesty, Hebe, Michaelmas daisy, Runner bean, Ice plant, Forget-me-not, Bramble, Seneccio, Honeysuckle

The Large White is probably the most widespread of all British butterflies and has been seen in almost every part, including as far north as Shetland. It is not generally seen until late April and there are few around in July, but the emergence of the summer brood together with the migrants from Europe makes this butterfly one of the commonest seen during August.

The **Red Admiral** is also a migrant from Europe and its numbers depend on weather conditions there. There are good Red Admiral years and bad years - 1996 was a good year, and as is often the case with migrants, the following year, 1997, was a bad year. A few Red Admirals hibernate in Britain during the winter, especially in the south and these may be seen flying in early spring.

Depending on the weather and wind direction migrants can start arriving on the south coast during March and then make their way northwards. They can fly as far north as Shetland. These migrants will breed on stinging nettles, so that Red Admirals seen later in the year may be either migrants or 'home-grown'. In the autumn this butterfly likes nothing better than to feed on rotting fruit and often dozens can be found under fruit trees. Earlier in the year they will be found feeding on buddleia.

Red Admiral

Favourite plants

Ice plant, Michaelmas daisy, Red valerian, Ivy, Hemp agrimony, Bramble, Field scabious, Aster, Lavender, Privet, Marjoram, Cotoneaster, Honeysuckle, Hydrangea

Small Tortoiseshell

Favourite plants

Ice plant, Michaelmas daisy, Aubretia, Lavender, Red valerian, Field scabious, Hebe, Marjoram, Candytuft, Lobelia, Mint, Hemp agrimony, Common fleabane, Wallflower, Verbena, Alyssum

Although most return south in the autumn it is possible to see a Red Admiral as late as December if the weather is warm.

For six years running our garden butterfly survey found the **Small Tortoiseshell** to be the most widespread species in gardens. This butterfly occurs throughout the British Isles and the late summer and autumn butterflies feed up on nectar, often from buddleia, though many flowers are used. They then hibernate during the winter to emerge in the spring, when they mate and lay eggs for the next generation. The Small Tortoiseshell has two generations in the south, with the first to emerge in late June breeding to produce a second generation in late August or September. Generally, there is only one generation in the north, where butterflies emerging in the summer do not breed but feed up and hibernate through the winter to emerge and breed in the spring.

Providing suitable butterfly habitats is simple to achieve in any garden

The **Peacock** also hibernates through the winter, but nature has cleverly staggered the emergences of this butterfly and its relative, the Small Tortoiseshell, so that each species feeds at a slightly different time: Peacocks in late July/early August and Small Tortoiseshells mid-August/September. By the time the mass of Small Tortoiseshells appears most of the Peacocks will have gone into hibernation, although there will always be a few individuals around until late Autumn.

It is one of the delights of late summer to see dozens of exotic-looking Peacocks gliding around the buddleias and other nectar plants and then later the more homely Small Tortoiseshells flitting amongst the flowers. If the buddleias have finished flowering then ice plant and Michaelmas daisy are favourites. Like its relatives, the Red Admiral and Small Tortoiseshell, the Peacock breeds on stinging nettles, but has just one brood per year. Although common in southern Britain this butterfly is rare in Scotland.

Peacock

Favourite plants

Ice plant, Michaelmas daisy, Aubretia, Hebe, Red valerian, Hemp agrimony, Field scabious, French marigold, Wallflower, Dandelion, Grape hyacinth, Verbena, Hyacinth, Hydrangea, Cone flower

LESS WIDESPREAD GARDEN BUTTERFLIES

This list contains ten species: Brimstone, Green-veined White, Orange Tip, Common Blue, Holly Blue, Painted Lady, Comma, Speckled Wood, Gatekeeper and Meadow Brown. Which of these you will get in your garden will depend on where you live and the habitat nearby, as several do not fly far.

Brimstones only occur in the southern half of mainland Britain and are scattered in Ireland. The sulphur-yellow males are usually the first to emerge from winter hibernation and can be seen as early as February on a warm day. They are the original butter-coloured insects from which the name 'butter-fly' was coined. There are two main flight periods: March to May and August to October but individuals can be seen in November and December if the weather is warm. In fact, it is possible to see a Brimstone flying in any month of the year, the only butterfly for which this is true, although to see one in January is very rare.

Green-veined White

Favourite plants

Lavender, Aubretia, Honesty, Marjoram, Field scabious, Forget-me-not, Sweet rocket, Lobelia, Red valerian, Candytuft, Dandelion

Brimstone

Favourite plants

Runner bean, Phlox, Primrose, Aubretia, Honesty, Red valerian, Wallflower, Michaelmas daisy, Cranesbill, Hyacinth

The Brimstone flies considerable distances, but to get it to stop in your garden you need bright flowers such as scarlet runner beans, everlasting pea or red phlox. The caterpillars feed on buckthorn bushes. These foodplants are easily grown in gardens, the females laying eggs on even the smallest bush and they have the amazing ability of finding even the most isolated trees.

The **Green-veined White** is a relative of the Large and Small Whites but it does not lay its eggs on brassicas, using wild or ornamental members of the cabbage family instead. It is particularly fond of garlic mustard and hedge mustard. If these are too much like weeds for your garden, then try growing lady's smock (cuckoo flower), another favourite foodplant plant also used by the Orange Tip. The Green-veined White is found throughout the British Isles (except Shetland) and is quite common in Scotland. It can generally be seen in gardens near woodland or other damp habitats in May and second brood adults in late July to mid-September.

Orange Tip

Favourite plants
Honesty, Aubretia, Forget-me-not, Sweet rocket

The **Orange Tip** is another relative of the whites and it uses some of the same caterpillar foodplants in gardens as the Green-veined White. It is particularly fond of lady's smock, honesty and sweet rocket (dame's violet). The Orange Tip can be found throughout England, Wales and Ireland. It is spreading from the east to other parts of Scotland and Butterfly Conservation is monitoring this butterfly closely here. If you have any records from Scotland please send them to the address on the back cover.

The first males with their conspicuous orange tips to the forewings are generally seen in late April and the flight period can extend to the beginning of July. Very occasionally there is a second brood in the south in late August.

Common Blue

Favourite plants
Marjoram, Lavender, Birds-foot-trefoil, Mint, Clover, Common fleabane, French marigold, Field scabious, Ice plant, Knapweed, Thyme, Hemp agrimony

The **Common Blue** occurs throughout Great Britain, reaching as far north as southern Shetland. Bird's-foot-trefoil is the favourite foodplant of the caterpillars and this pretty, low-growing plant is also a favourite nectar plant of the adults. I can never understand why this plant, with its orange/red and yellow 'pea' flowers has not been taken into cultivation. Admittedly it does spread and needs to be cut back during the growing season (at the end of July, when there are unlikely to be Common Blue eggs or caterpillars on the leaves).

There are two or even three broods of Common Blues per year in the south, but usually only one in the north. Adults can be seen flying from mid-May to the end of June/early July and again from August to mid-September.

Painted Lady

Favourite plants
Ice plant, Michaelmas daisy, Red valerian, Field scabious, Marjoram, Lavender, Hebe, Aster, Verbena, Dahlia

Where there is a third brood, adults can be seen as late as October. Common Blue is one of the few butterflies not to be much attracted to buddleia; you really need to grow bird's-foot trefoil, origanum (marjoram), lavender or the yellow common fleabane to attract this pretty butterfly to your garden.

Holly Blue

Photo: Ken Willmott

Favourite plants
Bramble, Forget-me-not, Hebe, Ivy, Marjoram, Escallonia

The **Holly Blue**, a relative of the Common Blue is a butterfly whose numbers ebb and flow, possibly due to its relationship with a parasitic wasp whose larvae eat the Holly Blue caterpillars. As parasite numbers build up Holly Blue numbers decline until they become too scattered for the wasp to find. At this point the numbers of the parasite fall and the Holly Blue starts to recover. Holly Blue caterpillars feed on holly and ivy flower buds.

Without the parasitic wasp it is likely that the numbers of caterpillars would build up to such an extent that the hollies and ivies would have no chance to set seed and they would die out. The Holly Blue could then be said to have caused its own extinction, so the parasite is very necessary to the survival of this species, although I miss this little piece of the sky flying round my garden during the years when numbers are very low.

Comma

Favourite plants
Ice plant, Michaelmas daisy, Bramble, Hebe, Ivy, Marjoram, Red valerian, Heather, Aster, Field scabious, Lavender, Privet

Holly Blues are only found in the southern half of Britain and around the Irish coast with a scattering inland. They are totally absent from Scotland. Adults can be seen flying from as early as the beginning of April in the south, but more usually late April to mid-June and then from July to September.

Speckled Wood

Favourite plants
Marjoram, Hebe, Field scabious, Honeysuckle

There is only one migrant from Europe and North Africa in the list of less widespread garden visitors: the **Painted Lady**. Its fortunes ebb and flow even more dramatically than those of the Red Admiral, with 1996 being an exceptionally abundant year. The early migrants start arriving in April if the wind is in the south, and breed here on thistles. The home-grown adults emerge to mix with a larger influx of migrants in August and this spectacular butterfly can be seen well into October. They migrate back to north Africa in the autumn.

To have visits from the **Comma** and **Speckled Wood** you need to have woodland or a thick hedge close to your garden, as these are their main breeding habitats and they do not fly far. The Comma is a relative of the

Small Tortoiseshell and Peacock and like them it hibernates as an adult during the winter and uses stinging nettles as the caterpillar foodplant. You need to live in the southern half of Britain to have a Comma visit as this species is not found in northern Britain or in Ireland.

The Speckled Wood is common in southern Britain and in Ireland but rare in northern Britain except for the south and west of Scotland. This species uses grasses as the caterpillar foodplant, but it is unlikely to breed in gardens, unless these are very large and have a woodland setting. Both Comma and Speckled Wood can be seen flying for three periods each year. Comma: April, July and autumn, when its favourite food is fruit juice from rotting fruit or blackberries.

Gatekeeper

Favourite plants

Marjoram, Bramble, Hebe, Hemp agrimony, Candytuft, Thyme, Common fleabane, Privet, Shasta daisy, Ragwort, Knapweed, Black-eyed Susan

Meadow Brown

Favourite plants

Marjoram, Field scabious, Lavender, Bramble, Hebe, Red valerian, Candytuft, Thyme, Privet, Common fleabane, Knapweed, Ice plant, Mint, Phlox

Speckled Wood: mid-April to mid-May, June and August to September. Both species have spread north in recent years, possibly due to climatic warming.

The females of the closely related **Gatekeeper** (Hedge Brown) and **Meadow Brown** lay their eggs on certain grasses, but are unlikely to be attracted to regularly mown grass. However, they will visit your garden for nectar. Gatekeepers, in particular, love origanum. Both are summer butterflies, the Meadow Brown adults being seen from late June to September and the Gatekeeper from mid-July to September. Meadow Brown can be seen throughout Great Britain, except the Shetlands, but Gatekeepers only occur in the southern half of Britain and in southern Ireland.

OCCASIONAL GARDEN BUTTERFLIES

Seven species belong to this category: Small Skipper, Large Skipper, Small Copper, Wall Brown, Marbled White, Small Heath and Ringlet.

As they were recorded in less than a third of gardens taking part in our survey, do not be too disappointed if you never see them in yours.

None of these species flies far, although in an exceptional year Marbled Whites can be seen some distance from the nearest colony.

You only have a chance of visits from these seven species if you have colonies nearby. However there are ways in which you can help to maintain and even create colonies and encourage all these species to visit your garden. They prefer wild flowers, such as knapweed, field scabious and common fleabane to garden varieties. Their infrequent visits to gardens make it hard to compile sufficient data for reliable lists of favourite plants.

The **Large Skipper** flies mainly in late spring and the **Small Skipper** in early summer, although both can be seen throughout the summer in England and Wales. Neither species oc-

Large Skipper

Small Heath

Small Skipper

Photo: Ken Willmott

Favourite plants

Lavender, Marjoram, Field scabious, Red valerian, Lobelia, Bramble, Sweet William, Candytuft, Hebe, Common fleabane

curs in Scotland or Ireland. Visits to gardens are rare and Small Skippers are more likely than Large.

It has been found from the survey that the **Small Copper** visits just under half of all gardens in a good year, but numbers can go down considerably in a year of bad weather.

This very pretty little butterfly occurs more or less throughout the British Isles and can have three broods in one season with adults flying in May, July-August and late September. It is very partial to yellow or white flowers with yellow centres, particularly common fleabane and ox-eyed daisy.

The **Small Heath** occurs throughout Great Britain, but is not a great garden visitor. There are two broods and adults fly in June and August - September. So few have been recorded feeding from garden plants that we have little idea what, if anything, attracts this tiny butterfly into a garden.

Small Copper

Favourite plants
Ice plant, Marjoram, Michaelmas daisy, Mint, Common fleabane, Field scabious, Thyme, Heather, Lavender, Hebe

Wall Brown

Favourite plants
Lavendar, Field scabious, Marjoram, Red valerian, Hebe

The **Wall Brown** is more likely to visit gardens in the north than those in the south, although it is rare in Scotland. It flies in May and in August with the possibility of a third brood in September in a good year in the south.

There are many more of these butterflies about in August than in May, and this is the month when they are most likely to visit gardens.

Finally, we have the **Marbled White** and the **Ringlet.** These two butterflies only occur in the southern half of Britain and are summer butterflies, with the Marbled White being seen a little earlier than the Ringlet.

The greatest numbers of both are seen in July and this is when they are most likely to visit gardens.

Marbled White

Butterfly distribution

In conclusion, it is important to note that each species of butterfly has a different distribution and range.

Ringlet

Nearly all of the 22 'garden species' occur in England and Wales, except in the higher mountain or hill ranges. Some will be found throughout the British Isles whereas others are restricted to more southern parts.

A few butterflies are migratory, such as the Red Admiral and the Painted Lady, so their location and numbers will vary greatly from one year to the next.

A rockery with aubretia in the foreground, wallflowers in the background

Reference to a good butterfly guide book with distribution maps will give you a fair idea as to which species you can expect to see in your particular garden.

FAVOURITE NECTAR PLANTS

There are nectar plants which attract many species of butterfly and others which seem to be favourites of just one species.

Every garden should contain the top ten nectar plants attracting the greatest number of butterflies, if at all possible, and it makes sense to also grow those plants which are the favourites of butterflies which visit your garden or which you have seen near by.

People often ask me why butterflies seen in a field or lane near to their garden never seem to visit. There are many reasons for this, but mainly it is because the garden is not attractive to that particular species.

By growing a favourite nectar plant in a sunny position you considerably increase your chance of visits from butterflies living nearby. As an example, I never saw a Gatekeeper in my garden until I started growing marjoram. Now I have two or three continuously feeding all through the summer.

The top ten favourite nectar plants

These include both cultivated plants and wild plants which can be obtained commercially.

If you have to make a choice, it is almost always better to grow the wild flowers, but there are at least ten cultivated plants which should be in all butterfly gardens: Buddleia; Ice plant; Lavender; Michaelmas daisy; Origanum (Marjoram); Aubretia; Red Valerian; French Marigold; Hebe and Candytuft.

These are described overleaf in order of their popularity, as found from our garden butterfly survey. *(See page 39 for a list of the top 100 plants for attracting butterflies.)*

Buddleia

The Butterfly Bush is by far the best nectar plant and is first favourite with 18 species: Brimstone, Comma, Common Blue, Gatekeeper, Green-veined White, Holly Blue, Large Skipper, Large White, Meadow Brown, Painted Lady, Peacock, Red Admiral, Small Copper, Small Skipper, Small Tortoiseshell, Small White, Speckled Wood and Wall Brown.

Buddleia

Buddleia had ten times as many reports of butterflies feeding on the flowers as any other plant, and it was found to be a favourite nectar source for 18 species of butterfly with 37 species reported as feeding on the flowers at some time.

It is a shrub stocked by most garden centres and there are several varieties available. Although the original light purple flowered variety seems to be the most consistent in attracting butterflies, all varieties do so to a greater or lesser extent. I have found self-sown seedlings to be particularly good.

More important than variety is the way you look after the shrub.

It must be planted in a sunny position and needs vigorous pruning in March to produce strong new growth. Well established bushes can be cut to less than half their size, although those newly planted should be treated more gently and just branches that have flowered cut back.

The bushes must be watered during drought periods, even those of only a few days during the flowering season, as nectar production requires ample supplies of water.

Normally, buddleia has quite a short flowering season but this can be extended by removing the dead spikes as they form. In some varieties this ensures a continuous flowering from July to September, in others it produces a second flowering in September, which is of great benefit to the autumn butterflies, particularly those that hibernate over the winter.

There are other species of buddleia which attract butterflies, probably the most useful is *B. weyeriana*, which starts to flower later and so takes over as a primary nectar source for autumn butterflies when *B.davidii* has finished flowering. The flowers are yellow with orange centres and occur on short spikes.

This species can grow into a very large bush and needs severe pruning in the spring, which also has the useful effect of postponing flowering until late summer. By removing the dead

White buddleia

spikes *B. weyeriana* will flower until the weather turns wintery.

Ice Plant

Ice Plant produces masses of small pink flowers in autumn which are rich in nectar and attract most butterflies which are around at this time, particularly Red Admiral, Small Tortoiseshell, Small Copper and Speckled Wood.

Altogether 25 butterfly species have been recorded feeding on the flowers during our survey. In some gardens it grows like a weed, but in others, particularly those not well-drained, it is more difficult to grow.

I have found that growing it in a pot of well-drained soil can be quite successful and has the advantage that you can move it around so that it is in the sun all the day, when it is in flower.

Lavender

Lavender is a real old cottage garden plant. Thirty butterfly species have been recorded feeding on the flowers and it is a particular favourite of the whites, including Green-veined White, while Common Blue and Wall Brown also favour this plant. It is best to buy the genuine, pale mauve, original lavender, not the various named varieties and low-growing shrubs stocked by many garden centres, as these will not have the same attraction.

Lavender

Lizzie Harper

To keep the bush vigorous it needs to be pruned every year during the winter and it can be encouraged to produce a partial second blooming by removing all the dead spikes after flowering.

Michaelmas Daisy

Michaelmas daisy is another autumn flowering nectar plant. It is a favourite nectar plant for Small Copper, Small Tortoiseshell and Speckled Wood and altogether 22 species have been recorded feeding on Michaelmas daisy.

There are many varieties available, but the best nectar plants are those that have been around for at least 50 years such as 'Barr's Pink'. Because the plants spread over the years they need dividing up from time to time, so gardeners are usually quite happy to give away unwanted plants and this is probably the best way of obtaining a variety which you know will attract butterflies.

Origanum (Marjoram)

Origanum or majoram is a plant grown in herb gardens for centuries and also occuring wild. This is the plant that will attract Gatekeepers to your garden and it is also a favourite of the Wall Brown, with 27 other species having been recorded feeding on it.

Most garden centres stock origanum in their herb section and as it is a plant that both spreads and seeds itself you only need to buy one to start with.

In a small garden origanum can be grown in pots or tubs very effectively. It is a plant that needs a lot of water during drought periods to keep it healthy.

Aubretia

Aubretia is a low growing, spreading plant with mauve flowers that blooms in the spring. It also often has a second blooming later in the year and altogether 21 species have been recorded as feeding on the flowers.

It is a particular favourite of the Small Tortoiseshell and Wall Brown in the spring.

Aubretia looks particularly attractive growing over banks and walls, when the small purple flowers spill over like a waterfall. As with all butterfly plants it should be planted in a sunny position.

Lizzie Harper

Marjoram

Red Valerian

It is the pink variety of the Red Valerian which seems to be the most attractive to butterflies, although I have had many Small Tortoiseshells feeding on the red flowers in the autumn.

This hardy perennial, which likes to grow in dry, stony ground also attracts moths such as the Silver-Y and 30 species of butterfly have been recorded as feeding on the flowers.

French Marigold

The single flowered varieties of the French marigold are the best for attracting butterflies and this annual is a favourite nectar plant of the summer butterflies, Common Blue, Comma and Meadow Brown before the buddleia comes into bloom, with 23 species having been recorded feeding on the flowers.

It is best to raise the seeds in a greenhouse, or to buy bedding plants in May, after all danger of frost has passed, as French marigolds are half-hardy. The very small flowered, single French marigold known as Tagetes 'Naughty Marietta' is less popular at garden centres but if it can be found is well worth buying, being very free-flowering and attractive to butterflies. It is easily grown from seed.

Hebe

Hebes are popular garden shrubs and are stocked by most nurseries and garden centres. You need to experiment to find the variety which is most attractive to the butterflies in your garden.

Hebe

Lizzie Harper

Overall, 26 species of butterfly have been seen on hebe and it is one of the few plants liked by the Speckled Wood. By cutting off the dead flowers early in the season you can often induce the shrub to flower again later.

Candytuft

Candytuft is a very variable butterfly attractant. In some years and in some gardens it would be classed as one of the best, in other years or in other gardens it has been found to be very poor. However, being a hardy annual which readily seeds itself it is easy to grow and well worth trying.

A possible explanation for its variableness is that its flowering season is not long and depends on when the seeds are sown and the weather, so that at times it may be flowering at the end of June when there are few butterflies around in gardens.

Over six years of the garden butterfly survey 26 species of butterfly have been recorded feeding on the flowers and it is a favourite of the Small Skipper, an early summer butterfly.

SOME CATERPILLAR FOODPLANTS

There are a number of plants worth growing to try to attract butterflies to breed in your garden, rather than simply to visit. Those listed below are also attractive plants to have in the garden.

Bird's-foot trefoil for the Common Blue
Holly for Holly Blue
Honesty for Orange Tip
Ivy for Holly Blue
Lady's smock for Orange Tip
Nasturtium for Large White and Small White
Sorrel for Small Copper
Sweet rocket for Orange Tip

However, if you have a wild area then some weeds are very useful to butterflies and will encourage them to breed in your garden.

Stinging nettles for the Small Tortoiseshell, Peacock, Red Admiral and Comma
Thistle for the Painted Lady
Bramble for nectar flowers

Peacock caterpillars feasting on stinging nettles

THE 100 BEST BUTTERFLY NECTAR PLANTS

in order of attraction

Buddleia
Ice plant
Lavender
Michaelmas daisy
Marjoram
Red valerian
Aubretia
Field scabious
Scabious
Bramble
French marigold
Hebe
Candytuft
Lobelia
Honesty
Mint
Hemp agrimony
Phlox
Forget-me-not
Aster
Sweet rocket
Runner bean
Knapweed
Privet
Purple loosestrife
Verbena
Alyssum
Common fleabane

Dandelion
Dahlia
Wallflower
Bowles mauve wallflower
Ivy
Heather
Shrubby cinquefoil
Ragwort
Cranesbill
Primrose
Tree mallow
Chives
Thyme
Catmint
African marigold
Pansy
Black eyed Susan
Hydrangea
Golden rod
Ox-eye daisy
Sweet William
Shasta daisy
Hyssop
Rock rose
Honeysuckle
Daisy
Teasel
Sneezewort
Chrysanthemum (single)
Cosmos, Cosmea
Osteospermum
Clover
Globe thistle
Marguerite
Pot marigold
Escallonia
Everlasting flower
Lilac

Cornflower
Hyacinth
Lychnis coronaria
Red campion
Nasturtium
Ceratostigma
Statice
Cone flower
Senecio
Onions
Virginia stocks
Petunia
Busy Lizzie
Coreopsis
Bluebell
Yarrow
Birds-foot- trefoil
Everlasting pea
Cuckoo flower
Feverfew
Inula
Pinks
Sneezeweed, Helenium
Flos flower, Ageratum
Corn marigold
Sea holly
Grape hyacinth
Cotoneaster
Buttercup
Hemp agrimony
Viola
Ceanothus
Musk mallow
Heliotrope

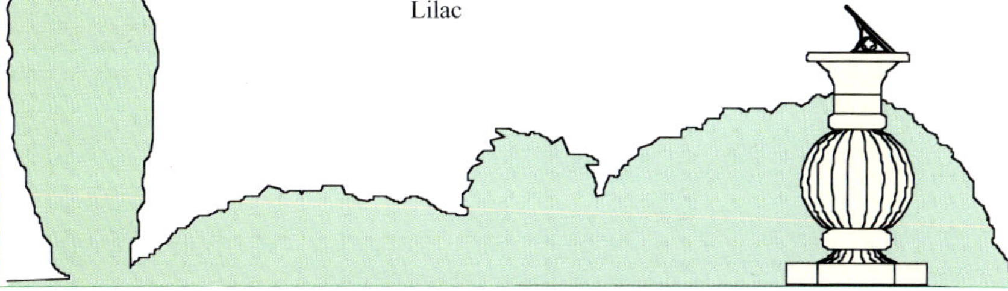

PROTECTING LOCAL HABITATS

It goes without saying that unless your garden is large enough and of the correct habitat to support a breeding colony, almost all butterfly visitors will have been born and bred elsewhere, mostly in nearby habitat.

These breeding habitats are extremely valuable, but also extremely vulnerable to destruction unless they are identified and protected.

To search out the places where your garden butterflies are breeding can be an exciting as well as a valuable pursuit.

Places to look for include deciduous woodland, rough grassland with abundant wild flowers, disused railway lines, road verges and land remaining after building work has been completed.

Abandoned industrial sites can be very good, even areas in parks, although here you will probably have to persuade the authorities to leave areas of grass uncut during the summer and not to treat stinging nettles with weedkiller.

The same goes for roadside verges, especially large corner areas where two roads meet.

If you do not feel confident enough to approach the authorities yourself enlist the help of your local Butterfly Conservation branch or county wildlife trust. You will need to produce evidence that the area is a good habitat for butterflies and to do this you need to visit regularly from April to September, preferably once a week and count the numbers of different butterflies you see, keeping a note of the results.

Make a note of any other interesting wildlife you see, too, such as birds or plants.

It is important to protect local habitats

A Comma butterfly feeds on a ripe blackberry - bramble flowers are also a good nectar source

Under Local Agenda 21, an initiative which followed the 1992 Rio Earth Summit, Local Authorities have a statutory duty to maintain the biodiversity in their area, which means protecting all forms of wildlife.

One of the ways they do this is to make an area good for wildlife into a Local Nature Reserve, which protects it from future development. Local Authorities have used their powers to aquire, declare and manage Local Nature Reserves since 1949. Often these areas are managed for wildlife in conjunction with the local wildlife trust or urban wildlife trust.

However, Local Authorities do not always have the manpower or expertise to go out looking for such areas, they need the public to tell them which pieces of land are worth protecting and to produce evidence to support the claim.

Continuous management is vital to keep the habitat suitable for the butterfly populations present and to attract colonising species. Local Authorities rarely have the time or funds to do this alone, often relying on volunteer help. It is a very worthwhile and rewarding experience to become a warden of a Local Nature Reserve. However, don't think that if you suggest an area for protection you will then have to become warden if it is made an LNR, this is purely voluntary.

It may be that you are lucky enough to live near a nature reserve already and this is the source of the butterflies that visit your garden.

To maintain suitable habitat the nature reserve requires continuous management (cutting down scrub, coppicing trees, scything grasses etc) and volunteers can often help - perhaps you could go to one or more workdays. Almost all Butterfly Conservation branches and county wildlife trusts arrange habitat management days, usually during the winter. This is a good way to make friends, get some exercise and warm up on a cold day and by helping to maintain their habitat you will make sure you have butterfly visitors in your garden the next spring and summer.

COMMON AND SCIENTIFIC NAMES OF PLANTS

African marigold	*Tagetes erecta*
Alyssum	*Alyssum*
Aster	*Aster*
Aubretia	*Aubretia deltoidea*
Birds-foot- trefoil	*Lotus corniculatus*
Black eyed Susan	*Rudbeckia fulgida*
Bluebell	*Endymion non-scriptus*
Bramble	*Rubus fruticosus*
Buddleia	*Buddleia*
Busy Lizzie	*Impatiens*
Buttercup	*Ranunculus*
Candytuft	*Iberis amara*
Catmint	*Nepeta*
Ceanothus	*Ceanothus*
Ceratostigma	*Ceratostigma willmottianum*
Chives	*Allium schoenoprasum*
Chrysanthemum (single)	*Chrysanthemum*
Clover	*Trifolium repens*
Common fleabane	*Pulicaria dysenterica*
Cone flower	*Echinacea purpurea*
Coreopsis	*Coreopsis tinctoria*
Cornflower	*Centaurea cyanus*
Corn marigold	*Chrysanthemum segetum*
Cosmos, Cosmea	*Cosmos*
Cotoneaster	*Cotoneaster*
Cranesbill	*Geranium*
Cuckoo flower	*Cardamine pratensis*
Dahlia	*Dahlia*
Daisy	*Bellis perennis*
Dandelion	*Taraxacum*
Escallonia	*Escallonia*
Everlasting flower	*Helichrysum bracteatum*
Everlasting pea	*Lathyrus latifolius*
Feverfew	*Tanacetum parthenium*
Field scabious	*Knautia arvensis*
Flosflower, Ageratum	*Ageratum*
Forget-me-not	*Myosotis*
French marigold	*Tagetes patula*
Globe thistle	*Echinops*
Golden rod	*Solidago*
Grape hyacinth	*Muscari*
Heather	*Erica*
Hebe	*Hebe*
Heliotrope	*Heliotropium*
Hemp agrimony	*Eupatorium cannabinum*
Honesty	*Lunaria annua*

Honeysuckle	*Lonicera periclymenum*
Hyacinth	*Hyacinthus orientalis*
Hydrangea	*Hydrangea macrophylla*
Hyssop	*Hyssopus officinalis*
Ice plant	*Sedum spectabile*
Inula	*Inula*
Ivy	*Hedera helix*
Knapweed	*Centaurea*
Lavender	*Lavandula angustifolia*
Lilac	*Syringa vulgaris*
Lobelia	*Lobelia*
Lychnis	*Lychnis coronaria*
Marguerite	*Chrysanthemum frutescens*
Marjoram	*Origanum vulgare*
Michaelmas daisy	*Aster novi-belgii*
Mint	*Mentha*
Musk mallow	*Malva moschata*
Nasturtium	*Tropaeolum majus*
Onions	*Allium*
Osteospermum	*Osteospermum*
Ox-eye daisy	*Leucanthemum vulgare*
Pansy	*Viola*
Petunia	*Petunia*
Phlox	*Phlox*
Pinks	*Dianthus*
Pot marigold	*Calendula officinalis*
Primrose	*Primula vulgaris*
Privet	*Ligustrum*
Purple loosestrife	*Lythrum salicaria*
Ragwort	*Senecio*
Red campion	*Silene dioica*
Red valerian	*Centranthus ruber*
Rock rose	*Helianthemum*
Runner bean	*Phaseolus multiflorus*
Sea holly	*Eryngium*
Senecio	*Senecio*
Shasta daisy	*Leucanthemum x superbum*
Shrubby cinquefoil	*Potentilla fruticosa*
Sneezeweed, Helenium	*Helenium*
Sneezewort	*Achillea*
Statice	*Psylliostachys suworowii*
Sweet rocket	*Hesperis matronalis*
Sweet William	*Dianthus barbatus*
Teasel	*Dipsacus fullonum*
Thyme	*Thymus*
Tree mallow	*Lavatera*
Verbena	*Verbena*
Viola	*Viola*
Virginia stocks	*Malcolmia maritima*
Wallflower	*Erysimum cheiri*
Yarrow	*Achillea millefolium*

USEFUL CONTACTS AND REFERENCES

PLANT AND SEED MERCHANTS

Bressingham Gardens, Bressingham, Diss, Norfolk, IP22 2AB (Herbaceous plants and shrubs)

DT Brown & Co Ltd, Station Road, Poulton-le-Fylde, Lancs FY6 7HX Orderline freephone: 0800 731 1231 (Seeds)

Naturescape, Lapwing Meadows, Coachgap Lane, Langar, Notts. NG13 9HP (Wild flower plants and seeds)

Sutton's Nurseries, Ledsham Lane, Lesham, South Wirral I66 0NB (Seeds)

Unwins Seeds Ltd, Histon, Cambridge CB4 4LE (Seeds)

John Chambers, 15 Westleigh Road, Barton Seagrave, Kettering, Northants. NN15 5AJ (Native British wildflower seeds)

W W Johnson & Sons Ltd, Stells Lane, London Road, Boston, Lincs, PE34 4RT (Native British wildflower seeds)

The Organic Gardening Catalogue, run jointly by HDRA and Chase Organics, offers seeds, plants and products and is available free from River Dene Estate, Molesey Road, Hersham, Surrey KT12 4RG

WHERE TO GO FOR ADVICE

Butterfly Conservation, PO Box 222, Dedham, nr Colchester, Essex, CO7 6EY (for general advice about butterflies and moths and their conservation)

County wildlife trusts (for advice on creating a wild area, planting hedges, peat-free gardening etc)

Henry Doubleday Research Association (HDRA), Ryton Organic Gardens, Coventry, CV8 3LG (organic gardening)

SOME USEFUL BOOKS

Thomas, Jeremy A, *Butterflies of the British Isles*, A Hamlyn Guide, 1996.

Heath, J, & Maitland Emmett, *The Butterflies of Britain and Ireland*, Harley Books, 1990.

Fry , R, *Habitat Conservation for Insects*, 1992, Amateur Entomologists Society.

Thomas, J & Lewington, R *The Butterflies of Britain & Ireland*, Dorling Kinderlsey 1991

Porter, J *Caterpillars of the British Isles* Viking 1997

Vickery, M, *Butterfly plants for the garden*, price £3, available from 3 The Deer Leap, Kenilworth, CV8 2HW.

Stevens, J, *National Trust book of wild flower gardening*, Dorling Kindersley, 1987.